LOOK UP!

Can you see
the sky sparkle and shine?
Up there live the Sun, the
Moon, and all the planets —
each one with a special job
to do.
The Sun helps us feel warm
and bright inside.
The Moon reminds us to rest
and dream.
The planets dance around
them,
teaching us about love,
courage, kindness, and
imagination.
Every planet is a friend,
and every friend has
something magical to share.
Let's meet them one by one —
and discover what makes
your little universe so
special!

I BRING WARMTH AND LIGHT.

I HELP EVERYTHING GROW, AND I REMIND YOU TO SHINE BRIGHT.

LOOK UP! I AM THE SUN..

I HEAL EMOTIONS.

WHEN YOU FEEL
SLEEPY OR SAD,
I GUIDE YOUR
HEART TO PEACE.

LOOK UP!
I AM THE MOON..

THE MOON

I LOVE TO TALK
AND THINK FAST.

I HELP YOU SHARE
YOUR THOUGHTS
AND LEARN NEW
THINGS EVERY DAY.

LOOK UP!
I AM MERCURY..

MERCURY

I AM BEAUTY AND LOVE.

I REMIND YOU TO BE KIND AND SEE THE LOVELY THINGS AROUND YOU.

LOOK UP!
I AM VENUS..

VENUS

I GROW PLANTS, TREES, AND ALL LIVING THINGS.

I LOVE IT WHEN YOU TAKE CARE OF ME.

LOOK UP!
I AM EARTH..

I AM BRAVE AND STRONG.

I HELP YOU TRY NEW THINGS AND STAND UP FOR YOURSELF.

LOOK UP!
I AM MARS..

MARS

I BRING LUCK AND GIFTS.

I HELP YOU DREAM BIG AND BELIEVE IN GOOD THINGS.

LOOK UP!
I AM JUPITER..

I HAVE SHINY RINGS AND LOTS TO TEACH.

I REMIND YOU THAT PRACTICE MAKES YOU GREAT.

LOOK UP!
I AM SATURN..

SATURN

I LOVE TO DO THINGS DIFFERENTLY.

I SHOW YOU IT'S FUN TO BE UNIQUE.

LOOK UP
I AM URANUS!

URANUS

I DREAM AND IMAGINE.

I HELP YOU BELIEVE IN MAGIC AND LISTEN TO YOUR HEART.

LOOK UP!
I AM NEPTUNE..

NEPTUNE

The Sun and
the planets all shine for you.

They remind you that every
feeling, every dream,
and every moment is part of
your bright, beautiful
universe.
When you feel happy or sad,
brave or shy,
just look up and remember –
the stars are cheering you on.
You are made of the same light
that fills the sky.
Keep shining, keep dreaming,
and keep being wonderfully,
perfectly you!

LOOK UP!

© 2025 21st Moon. All rights reserved.

Published by Moon Publishing
All rights reserved. No part of this publication may be reproduced, stored, or transmitted in any form or by any means —electronic, mechanical, photocopying, recording, or otherwise —without prior written permission of the publisher.

Printed in the United Kingdom
ISBN: 9781919336220
Cover and design by 21" Moon